# Rich Man, Poor Man

## How Money Controls Men's Mating Options

### Shanelle Shalom

# Rich Man, Poor Man: How Money Control Men's Mating Options

Written by Shanelle Shalom

August 2024

Queens of Virtue Relationship & Femininity Coaching

www.qovcoaching.com

# INTRODUCTION

# MONEY & MATING

I'm elated that I finally found an excuse to discuss my two favorite topics in one book—*relationships* and *money*. These two things are so important because both give humans something to fall back on when life gets rough. Relationships provide us with a support system, and money provides us with security. To me, and to a few other women out there, relationships and money go hand-in-hand. We are known to factor in a man's financial standing into our dating preferences, but it's debatable if men take these preferences seriously. Possibly because both rich and poor men get their share of women, despite their huge financial differences. This gives the impression that finances are irrelevant to mating options, but that can't be further from the truth.

In *Rich Man, Poor Man: How Money Controls Men's Mating Options*, we will discuss the advantages and disadvantages you face, or *may* face, because of your financial standing. This is important to discuss because a man's financial status usually changes at some point during his lifetime. You will need to know what to expect if or when your finances change, because your options will change along with it. Throughout this book, I will be using the terminology "rich" and "poor", but I am referring to men who are doing well financially versus men who are average and below. Neither may be rich or poor, per se, but they will be categorized that way for the sake of the book. Let's get started, shall we?

# THEY *Date* THEM ALL

Have you ever noticed that many of the women who desire rich men spend the majority of their time with men who aren't? Some never even been around rich men before, but somehow, they have become their preference. They don't know anything about them other than they can provide security and a lifestyle. But that is all they *need* to know in order for rich men to become a preference.

Financial security is a big deal for women for multiple reasons. First, it eliminates much of their anxieties about survival. They won't have to worry about how they will shelter, clothe, and feed themselves. Secondly, they can have babies with peace of mind, knowing that while they are dedicating their time to taking care of the children, the children's survival needs are taken care of. Third, finances provide them and their children with a higher social status. Women are extremely concerned about their public image, and status improves their image in the eyes of others. Women also have a competitive side, and status places them "above" other women. Lastly, financial security provides women (and their children) with a privileged lifestyle. They can live in better neighborhoods, send their children to better schools, live in nicer houses, and have experiences (such as traveling, vacations, etc.) that others do not.

A woman doesn't have to be with a rich man or be around them to know that she wants these benefits. However, she may still date *poor* men because they come with benefits also. Attention, being the biggest one. Women love to feel like they are the one and only girl in the world who matters, but a man who has lots of money is hardly giving his attention to only one woman. Even if he is, lots of his attention will go to his job or business. It's likely that a woman who loves attention won't be able to deal with this for long.

Another benefit that poor men provide is security through monogamy—at least, this is what women *think*. Poor men can't provide financial security, so they're expected to secure their woman in other ways. We all know that men who don't have money also cheat, but the fact that they don't have a financial advantage makes it less likely that they will be unfaithful, simply because they don't have the options that rich men have. It could also be argued that a rich man may view women as more disposable than poor men, but that is up for debate.

So, who gets the better woman, or better *treatment* from women—the rich man or the poor man? It all depends on which qualities are a woman's highest priority. If attention and emotional security is her highest priority, then the poor man would probably be her preference. If a privileged lifestyle and financial security is her priority, then the rich man would be her preference. It may be helpful to know that most women prefer emotional security over financial security, that is why an average man with average income and average looks can still get married and have children. He may not be able to provide an opulent lifestyle, but he can provide a lifestyle that is good enough to secure himself and his family. Most women are satisfied with this.

The question would now be, what kind of woman is *your* preference? Women have their preferences and I'm sure you have yours, too. Your income can assist you with getting the women you prefer. The higher your income, the wider range of women you can have. Why? Because *you* are the preference once you have some extra money in your pocket. Women aren't typically concerned about looks, height, and personality when the man in question has money. They will overlook many things that were once a preference before and prioritize his finances instead.

Once you become the preference, you will then get access to your own preferences. But it's hard to do this with no money. Less money equals less options, and less options equals less access to preferences. But again, it all depends upon what your preferences are. You may not prefer anyone that requires that you have financial success. But let's be honest here—all men have a "dream girl" and the dream girl is usually out of your league. She wouldn't even notice your existence. However, if you had a larger bank account, she might.

"THE POOR IS HATED EVEN OF HIS OWN NEIGHBOR: BUT THE

RICH HATH MANY FRIENDS."
~PROVERBS 14:20

# THEY *Date* THEM ALL ASSIGNMENT

This section is designed to help you do some self-reflection about your current state of mind and future goals when it comes to money and mating. You can write your answers down in a notebook if you need them for future reference.

1. Do you believe money plays a significant part in a man's attractiveness? Why or why not?

2. Are you currently satisfied with your dating options? Why or why not?

3. Have you noticed that men who have more or less money than

you have a different dating experience than you?

4. Do you know any women who are in a relationship with a rich man? Do they seem happy?

5. What is your ideal income? Do you believe you will one day have this income?

6. Has a woman ever dated you for your money? If so, what did you learn from that experience?

7. Do you desire a "dream girl?" Do you need to have money in order to have her?

# FOR THE *Love* OF MONEY

Women see value in both poor and rich men, and men see value in both modest women and gold diggers. Oh, yes, you do. And when I get done explaining, you will agree with me. You may not like that gold diggers are more focused on a man's money than his heart, but that doesn't mean there aren't other things about them you like.

For one, gold diggers are *usually* visually appealing. A man can appreciate a woman who keeps up her image, am I right? Gold diggers know that men with money have access to the best, so they make sure they look their best to appeal to them. They also receive financial benefits from these men, which provides them with the funds to invest in the best beauty treatments and attire to look more appealing than the average woman. Even if a man doesn't like the idea of a woman being a gold digger, he can't deny the beauty of one.

Gold diggers also have more confidence than the average woman. This is usually because they've been "poured into" instead of "taken from". What I mean is, the men they date give them a more privileged experience than most women, so they don't carry the resentment that other women carry towards men. There is a type of resentment that women build up by dealing with men who can't give them anything but are always willing to take. They take time, attention, sacrifice, sex, and sometimes money from these women. Women are in a constant state of giving when they are with poor men. The only thing these men *can* give is attention and sex, which is only enough for a time. Eventually, a woman begins to develop a desire for more. Women who receive provisions from men are always going to exude more positive energy than women who are giving to men, but rarely ever receiving.

Another attractive trait gold diggers have is a higher sense of self-worth. They do not put up with the same things other women do. Women who date poor men are not only dealing with his lack of money, but they are dealing with his other problems as well. He may be selfish, insensitive, inconsiderate, a liar or cheater, as well as broke. The lack of finances is rarely the *only* problem poor men have. Yet, the women who date them put up with *all* their problems for as long as they possibly can. Gold diggers wouldn't put up with such a thing. If a man is going to have all those problems, he better have enough money to make up for it! Gold diggers refuse to go through those challenges for free because they feel they are worth more.

Being physically appealing, confident, and exuding self-worth are all attractive traits regardless of whether a woman is a gold digger or not. It just so happens that gold diggers are the ones who consistently display these traits, and rightfully so. Provision definitely has an effect on women, financially and mentally. There is a level of peace and comfort that comes with being provided for. A woman who has bills and expenses hanging over her head is not going to give off the same energy as a woman who doesn't have to worry about that.

Provision can bring out some of the better qualities in a woman. This is hard for some of you to fathom because *your* better qualities are usually brought out by challenges, hard work, and responsibilities. These things make you stronger, more disciplined, and strategic. But this isn't the case for women. Women become cranky, exhausted, and aggressive when they have too many challenges and responsibilities. They become a more pleasant version of themselves when their load is lightened.

If you happen to marry by the age of 25, you most likely won't have much resources, so you will have to build your financial stability with the help of your wife. But at some point, hopefully sooner than later, you should be able to fully provide for your family without financial help from your wife. If she's forced to help you make money for more than five years into the marriage, she will begin to build up resentment about it. Women usually want to start having children a couple of years after they get married, and they should have the privilege of staying home to take care of the baby. They shouldn't have to work while they're pregnant, and then go right back to work after maternity leave. If your wife has to do this, she will begin to resent you for not having the money to allow her to do what comes natural to her—to stay home with her baby.

If you want your wife to view you as a leader, you must become financially independent. Unless she genuinely enjoys working and making money, she will soon come to a point where she no longer wants to work full time. She will expect you to be able to hold it down yourself. You become more respectable in her eyes when you show that you are capable. Here's a secret that many men don't know: **Women prefer men who don't need a woman**. They are more willing to be a help meet to you if you are the type of man to get the job done regardless of whether a woman is there to support you. As I mentioned earlier, if you marry young, you have no choice but to build everything with the help of your wife. But the downside to this is your wife won't get to see you accumulate anything on your own. She may question in the back of her mind if you have it in you to make things happen without her.

> "A GRACIOUS WOMAN RETAINS HONOR: AND STRONG MEN RETAIN RICHES." ~PROVERBS 11:16

# FOR THE *Love* OF MONEY | ASSIGNMENT

This section is designed to help you do some self-reflection about your current state of mind and future goals when it comes to money and mating. You can write your answers down in a notebook if you need them for future reference.

1. Have you ever dated a gold digger before? If so, what was the experience like?

2. What do you dislike about gold diggers? What do you like about gold diggers?

3. Has a woman ever financially taken care of you? If so, why?

4. Do you find a woman's confidence sexy or off-putting? Explain.

5. Do you *need* a woman? Why or why not?

6. What was the worst thing you've ever done for money?

7. Did you grow up poor? If so, did it shape your perspective of money?

# MONEY, *Power*, RESPECT

It's important that all men, no matter if they're rich or poor, have some type of advantage that other men don't have so that they may maintain a competitive edge in the dating market. Some men's advantage is their gift of gab, or charm. For some, it's their knowledge. Some have an advantage because of their skillset, and others because of their good looks. And of course, some men's advantage is their money. The great thing about this is that *all* these things are legitimate advantages. How far these advantages will take them depends upon how they use them. Do you know what your advantages are? If not, you should find out. There is an assignment at the end of this section that will help you discover your strengths.

Your advantages should get you the results you want, and hopefully, the results you want extend beyond sex. If you're only trying to get sex, be aware that it doesn't mean that you will get the woman's *respect*, which is technically more important than sex. Let's be frank, getting sex nowadays is not that hard because women are giving it up with less requirements. But do these women *respect* the men they are having sex with? Men place so much emphasis on sex that they aren't concerned about whether they are viewed as upstanding men. This is a travesty, but men are not solely the blame. Women must get back to showing sexual restraint. It's hard to get men to prioritize the right things while they are getting sex upfront. Whatever advantage you have in the dating market, be honest with yourself about if this advantage is only getting you laid, but nothing else. If so, then it's time to create a new game plan. Every man needs leverage. Money makes great leverage because money provides women with an experience that they can't provide themselves, and because other women want provision also, it places women in a position to compete for the men who can provide. But money is not the only form of leverage. Anything that gives you power or dominance in your relationship is leverage. The issue is men, even those with money, don't always know how to wield their power in a way that garners respect. Poor men are hip to this, so much so that they have a fear that if they were to be providers to a woman, she would only consume the resources without ever giving them the proper respect that he deserves. This problem is easily prevented.

If only men required women to show natural acts of love and respect *before* they provide, they would not have to worry about being used for their money. The typical courting process in America entails a man pursuing a woman, impressing her by putting his best foot forward, taking her on dates, and being charismatic and chivalrous. The woman, in turn, is to keep herself looking beautiful, sexy, and using her feminine charm to keep him interested in continuing to pursue. However, this game of cat and mouse doesn't require any noble acts from either party. Neither are showing good character. They're just going through the same motions that they went through several times before.

The truth of the matter is when a woman *likes* a man, she may do one thing, but when she *respects* a man, she will do another. These two emotions are not the same. Oftentimes, when men are courting a woman, they are only looking to be liked. But a woman can like a man and not respect him. If she likes you, it is because she finds your personality appealing, but that doesn't mean she takes you seriously as a person. It doesn't mean she wants your leadership, trusts your judgment, or believes you can make her life better than she can make it on her own. It doesn't mean she views you as an honorable member of society. It doesn't mean she thinks the world is better with you in it. Do you get my drift? *Like* doesn't equal *respect*.

You must start looking for signs of *respect* instead of signs of *like*. First, look for unsolicited loving gestures. In the beginning stages of a courtship, you want to see what your woman is willing to do to impress you without you asking. For example, let's say you take her on a date. If she brings you a small gift, such as a container of cupcakes she made from scratch, or a unique figurine that you can put on your desk at work, this shows that she's thoughtful and wants to be a positive presence in your life. Another thing to look for is consideration of your opinion. If she asks what you think about something and actually listens and engages with you without arguing, this is a sign that she has a genuine interest in your thoughts.

Another sign is refusal to interrupt you when you're speaking, which is a very simple, yet major sign of respect.

No woman should have instant access to your money, no matter how much or how little you have. Taking a woman out on *one* courtesy date may be appropriate, but continuously treating her to niceties while she hasn't shown any of the signs above is not going to get you any respect. If more men went by this rule of thumb, they could protect themselves from being used for money. If money is your leverage, your woman must be aware that full provision is conditional. You are scripturally obligated to provide your wife with food, shelter, and clothing, but you are not obligated to take her to fancy restaurants, buy her designer bags, or take her to get her nails done. These are luxuries that you can revoke from a disrespectful wife.

"HE THAT LOVES PLEASURE SHALL BE A POOR MAN: HE THAT LOVES WINE AND OIL SHALL NOT BE RICH." ~PROVERBS 21:17

# MONEY, *Power*, RESPECT

## ASSIGNMENT

This section is designed to help you do some self-reflection about your current state of mind and future goals when it comes to money and mating. You can write your answers down in a notebook if you need them for future reference.

1. Do you know what your greatest strengths are? If so, what are they? If not, answer these questions to help you find out...
   - What problems did you face in life that were reasonably easy for you to solve?
   - What ideas do you believe in that motivates you to act?

- What traits do you get the most compliments on?
- What personality traits do you find yourself using every day at work?
- Do you tend to be the teacher, or do you tend to be the student?
- Are you good with money? Are you financially literate?

2. Do women respect you? If so, what do they respect about you? If not, why don't they respect you?

3. If you had more money, would you feel more powerful? Would you feel more respectable?

4. What makes you feel powerful? What makes you feel respected?

5. Do you have respect for rich men? If so, what do you respect about them? If not, why don't you respect them?

# *Mind* OVER *Money*

What truly makes a man rich or poor is his mindset, more so than his income. His goals, character, morals, principles, wisdom, self-esteem, standards, and relationship with God makes him a rich man even if he currently doesn't have a dime to his name. I'm a firm believer that if a person has spiritual wealth, it is only a matter of time before it manifests to physical form. Besides, women's biggest complaint about men is not that you guys don't have enough money, but that you don't treat them the way they want to be treated. You will go much further with women if you learn how to treat them well (but not to your own detriment) while having an average income, than if you treated them poorly but had a high income.

The worse you treat women, the more money they desire you to have. They want you to have something to make up for your shortcomings. If you don't plan on making lots of money, then be an upstanding man so you won't have to. This doesn't mean you shouldn't have a financial standard for yourself, however. You still have to take care of yourself and your family. Determine how large you want your family to be, then determine how much money you will need to make to support them. You should not aspire to have less than you need to live comfortably. And be mindful that just because a woman doesn't need you to be rolling in dough doesn't mean she's okay with struggling financially.

Your financial goals should be considered when you are picking a mate. Men oftentimes choose who is compatible with them according to where they are in life at the time, but not necessarily where they are headed. The man who was poor but gets rich may no longer have the same attraction to his wife that he had when he was in a different state of mind. He also may not have as much time and attention to give to his wife as he used to, but his wife may still desire the attention he once gave. A rich man may choose a woman who loves the lifestyle he can provide her, but if he loses his high income, she will still want to live the same lifestyle she once had, but he won't be able to provide it. This is why you must be mindful of where you're going in life and choose a woman who can adapt to changing conditions.

# *Mind* OVER *Money*
## ASSIGNMENT

This section is designed to help you do some self-reflection about your current state of mind and future goals when it comes to money and mating. You can write your answers down in a notebook if you need them for future reference.

1. If you had $1,000,000 today, would you still make your wife go to work? Why or why not?

2. On a scale from 1 to 10, how well do you treat women? (1 being Horribly and 10 being Wonderfully)

3. What can you do to begin treating women better?

4. What are the top three most important traits that you look for in a woman?

5. What are your top three biggest fears when it comes to dating/relationships?

6. How many children do you want? Do you aspire to make enough money to take care of that many children?

7. Do you understand the purpose of provision? If so, what is its purpose? If not, see next chapter.

# THE *Purpose* OF *Provision*

1 Timothy 5:8 says, *"But if any provide not for his own, and specially for those of his own house, he hath denied the faith, and is worse than an infidel."* The definition of *infidel* is "a person who doesn't believe in religion or adheres to a religion other than his own". Refusing to provide for your family is a form of disloyalty. Disloyalty to God first and foremost, and disloyalty to your family secondly. God is a provider to those who are under his leadership (us), and you misrepresent him when you don't provide for those who are under *your* leadership (your

family). You were appointed to be the head of the family (1 Corinthians 11:3), but you distort your family's perspective of God when you don't display his attributes.

The actions of the father in the home influences the perspective of the Father in heaven. This is why it's so important for men to be involved in their children's lives and set a good example for them. One way that a father can set a great example is by upholding Proverbs 13:22, which says, *"A good man leaves an inheritance to his children's children, but the wealth of the sinner is stored up for the righteous."* Men sometimes get so wrapped up in whether they need money to get women that they don't see the purpose of having money past that point. Getting the woman isn't even half the battle. Your responsibilities as a man are much greater than simply getting a woman. You must minister to your wife and children by being a representative of God.

Your provision is a form of protection. It prepares your family for life's unforeseen circumstances. Sometimes emergencies happen. Unexpected bills show up. Someone suddenly gets sick. A tire is blown. Things happen that we don't expect but being financially stable takes care of these things. Finances also protects us when a crisis strikes, such as natural disasters or pandemics. Having extra money put away will allow you to move your family to safety or feed them when prices are inflated. There are many people who suffer because they simply didn't have the money to protect themselves or their family from something they had no control over. The world is cruel, but there are small hacks that make it less cruel, and money is one of those hacks.

Money, however, isn't the only way to provide. Being self-sufficient, like growing your own food, making your own clothing, or creating anything that you are used to buying will save you money and keep you from having to rely on big corporations to provide it for you. It would've benefited families all over the world if we had our own food garden when Corona Virus struck. We would've been able to feed ourselves instead of making several trips to the grocery store looking for goods. It was the pandemic that made me begin growing my own food. I felt so unprepared when it hit, but it made me want to learn some survival skills in case another unexpected crisis happened.

When you think of provision, don't only think of the financial purpose of it, but the spiritual significance as well. Having money isn't about giving your wife the ability to go on shopping sprees every weekend. Money takes financial worries off your family's mind. You won't have to spend time trying to figure out how you're going to take care of your basic needs. You can move on to other more important concerns. Think of it like Maslow's Hierarchy of Needs where the very basic needs are at the bottom of the pyramid. Once those basic needs are taken care of, you can focus on the needs one level above, and so on.

You may be happy with just the basics, and that's fine. To be frank, I believe most men are happy with just the basics. But men who have managed to get themselves past the basic level have eliminated at least one worry from their life, and if they have a wife and children, they've eliminated the worry from their lives also. Nobody really wants to worry about finances forever. They want to get to a point where they can relax, retire, and leave something behind for their children to inherit when they're gone. It isn't fair that children are forced to have financial concerns at an early age when they see their parents struggling and living paycheck to paycheck. Parents do their children an enormous favor by being financially stable.

Money has its place in this world. It's to *help* take care of us, our family, and give us the most comfortable lifestyle possible. Money isn't all we need, but it's definitely helpful to have. It's up to you to decide if money will or won't be a priority in your life. This book was only to help you make that decision. Thank you for reading *Rich Man, Poor Man*. I wish you the best of luck in your relationship life. I pray that you find a woman who loves and cares for you for a lifetime, for richer or poorer.

# *Purpose* of *Provision*
## ASSIGNMENT

This section is designed to help you do some self-reflection about your current state of mind and future goals when it comes to money and mating. You can write your answers down in a notebook if you need them for future reference.

1. After reading *Rich Man, Poor Man*, do you feel like you have a better understanding on how money effects mating?

2. Do you now have a better understanding of the spiritual

and financial significance of provision?

3. Do you want to provide for your wife? Why or why not?

4. Do you believe money is evil? Why or why not?

5. Are you a proper representation of what God intended for husbands/fathers?

6. Are you clear about the role a man plays in the household?

7. What was the most profound thing you learned in this book?

8. Was there anything in *Rich Man, Poor Man* that you disagreed with? If so, what part and why?

9. Would you recommend this book to another man?

# A SNEAK PREVIEW OF

"The tips found in this book is in no way new or trendy. They are classic and have been practiced since biblical times. It was effective then, and it is effective now. These tips have been taken straight out of the book of Esther. If you are not familiar with her story, Queen Esther was chosen to be the wife of King Ahasuerus after his first wife, Vashti, rebelled against him, causing her to lose her inheritance and royal crown—both in which were given to Esther instead. During her reign, Queen Esther, who was a Jew, was informed that it was requested that the Jewish citizens of their country be killed. To stop it, she put her life on the line by entering the King's chamber unsolicited and unannounced to plea her case for her people. Because she honored him, he gave the Queen half his kingdom and anything else she asked for. Esther was able to save the lives of her people, get them a national holiday, had the Jews' enemies killed, and get her cousin promoted to a high position in the kingdom, all while keeping her position as Queen and maintaining favor in the eyes of her husband. Not one time did Esther have to use any type of trickery to get what she wanted. All she had to do was be virtuous and courageous. She had *real* worth that was recognized by her King, and was able to get everything she wanted because of it.

Esther tapped into her virtue and femininity and allowed it to take her straight to the top while doing a good deed for others in the process. But she could not have had this level of power and influence on the King if she wasn't first chosen to be his wife. She did not work her magic outside of wedlock. Therefore, a virtuous woman like yourself, has to practice hypergamy by first preparing yourself to be a *wife* to a husband who can cover you completely. That means that he must be able to do three things: preach, provide, and protect. *Preach,* meaning that he must be able to educate you and his children. Of course, this includes educating you about God, scripture, prayer etc. *Provide* means that he must be able to materially and financially produce resources for you and his children. And *protect* means he must keep you and his children out of harm's way to the best of his ability—including putting his life on the line for you, if need be. You do not want to be with a man who thinks that his masculine duties are optional, because most likely, he will not see your feminine duties as optional. He would want you to be the full package, so he has to be as well.

The type of men that hypergamous coaches teach women to aim for are not the type we are aiming for in *Hypergamous Femininity*. We are not about getting the *wealthiest* man we can get. We're about getting the most *righteous* man we can get, because a righteous man will give us *all* of the things listed above."

www.ingramcontent.com/pod-product-compliance
Lightning Source LLC
Chambersburg PA
CBHW072018230526
45479CB00008B/282